Managing
Crises

Pocket Mentor Series

The *Pocket Mentor* Series offers immediate solutions to common challenges managers face on the job every day. Each book in the series is packed with handy tools, self-tests, and real-life examples to help you identify your strengths and weaknesses and hone critical skills. Whether you're at your desk, in a meeting, or on the road, these portable guides enable you to tackle the daily demands of your work with greater speed, savvy, and effectiveness.

Books in the series:

Managing
Crises

Expert Solutions to
Everyday Challenges

Harvard Business Press

Boston, Massachusetts

No part of this publication may be reproduced, stored in or introduced into a re-
trieval system, or transmitted, in any form, or by any means (electronic, mechanical,
photocopying, recording, or otherwise), without the prior permission of the pub-
lisher. Requests for permission should be directed to permissions@hbsp.harvard.edu,
or mailed to Permissions, Harvard Business School Publishing, 60 Harvard Way,
Boston, Massachusetts 02163.

Library of Congress Cataloging-in-Publication Data
Managing crises : expert solutions to everyday challenges.
     p. cm. — (Pocket mentor series)
   Includes bibliographical references.
   ISBN-13: 978-1-4221-2274-7
   1. Crisis management.
   HD49.M35 2008
   658.4'056—dc22

                              2007048565

The paper used in this publication meets the requirements of the American National
Standard for Permanence of Paper for Publications and Documents in Libraries and
Archives Z39.48-1992.

Contents

Mentor's Message: The Power of Effective Crisis Management

What would you do if your best employee quit tomorrow? What if your office building caught on fire and you were unable to access your computer or files for weeks—or worse, you lost your personal desktop files altogether? Would you be able to continue to do your job and keep your commitments to your customers, vendors, and contractors?

Many people think of crisis management as a job for internal audit groups, senior executives, and public relations professionals. And it's true in part—crises such as product tampering, food contamination, or fraudulent earnings reports are best handled by these people. But there are other unplanned events that could have a devastating impact on your group and organization. Crises such as a vendor's failing to complete a critical deliverable or the long-term illness of a crucial staff member could make it difficult or impossible for you to carry out your business operations.

But with good planning, you can minimize the impact of a potential disaster, avoid one altogether—or, in some cases, even help your company benefit from a crisis.

This guide lays out a process that can help you manage crises effectively, whether you're a company executive, division or unit manager, or team leader.

Norman R. Augustine, Mentor

Norman R. Augustine is chairman of the Executive Committee, Lockheed Martin; he formerly served as chairman and CEO of Lockheed Martin Corporation; director of Black & Decker, Phillips Petroleum, and Procter & Gamble; and undersecretary for the U.S. Army during the Vietnam War. He is the author of *Augustine's Laws* (Viking Penguin, 1986) and "Managing the Crisis You Tried to Prevent" (*Harvard Business Review*, 1995).

Managing Crises:
The Basics

What Is
a Crisis?

A CRISIS IS A CHANGE—sudden or evolving—that results in an urgent problem that must be addressed immediately. A crisis can occur in many forms:

- Life-threatening product defects are discovered.

- Computer hackers shut down a company's entire system and deny access to customers.

- A hard freeze destroys a region's citrus crops.

- A terrorist attack destroys lives and property.

- A key manager dies with no immediate replacement.

Crises are *not* the normal ups and downs of a business cycle—those recurring problems faced in the course of taking risks and exploring new avenues of opportunities. Instead, crises are wrenching, painful events. Yet some good can come out of these difficult experiences. The learning that comes from dealing with a crisis contains the seeds for future success in crisis prevention, crisis management, and, in some cases, even new opportunities.

In this section, you'll learn more about four types of crises: natural or company-related events, technology breakdowns, economic and market forces, and business-relationship crises.

"A crisis is an event that can affect or destroy an entire organization."
—Ian Mitroff

Natural or company-related events

Two types of crises fall in the category of natural or company-related events: uncontrollable natural events and health and environmental disasters related to a company.

An *uncontrollable natural event* of catastrophic magnitude can strike unexpectedly. This event may take the form of an earthquake, typhoon, tornado, hurricane, blizzard, flood, fire, or some other natural disaster that crushes buildings, destroys infrastructures, and interrupts communications.

A *health and environmental disaster related to a company* is a disastrous event that, though not necessarily *caused* by a company, is directly related to the company. The company is either responsible or perceived to be responsible for dealing with it. For example:

- An outside tampers with your company's product in a way that not only harms consumers but also damages the overall image of your product and company.

- Serious product problems come to light, such as defective tires or food contamination, for which your company does bear responsibility.

- Catastrophic accidents, such as major oil spills or radiation leakage, occur on your company's watch.

- Environmental pollution is unknowingly caused by your company in years past. For example, toxic waste with long-lasting harmful effects on wildlife and human health has been dumped into waterways.

What Would YOU Do?

What, Me Worry?

C AL IS THE MANAGER for a successful chain of retail stores. Over the past year, business has been booming. Earnings are up, and profit margins are growing. Because business has been so positive, Cal was surprised when he received a memo from the company's vice president asking him to perform a crisis audit. What did the vice president mean by a *crisis audit*? And why did Cal have to worry about a crisis when business was going so well? Cal didn't have a clue where to begin.

What would YOU do? The mentor will suggest a solution in *What You COULD Do*.

Technology breakdowns

Everyone knows what it's like when a company's server goes down. In this information age, we are extraordinarily dependent on technology to communicate, store information, do research, buy, and sell. Business today could not function without technology. Here are some common technological problems that could turn into crises:

- **Data loss.** Most companies in the United States do not have data backup plans. According to a University of Texas study, only 6 percent of companies that undergo major data loss will survive that crisis.

- **Security breaches.** A 2001 survey run by the Federal Bureau of Investigation and the Computer Security Institute revealed that 85 percent of large companies and government agencies have detected computer breaches in the past year. Moreover, while most computer attacks come from outside, attacks from inside cause the greatest financial loss.

- **Communications technology.** A retailer's Web site goes offline during the busiest season, stalling orders and frustrating customers and service representatives. A virtual team's Web site goes down, making it impossible for team members to meet a critical deadline. An entire phone system goes out, so that no one in the organization can receive or make calls except on their mobile phones.

- **Outmoded equipment.** When people work on aging equipment or on failing networks, they face a series of ongoing, minor crises every day—inefficient working conditions, difficulty meeting deadlines, lost e-mails, constant frustration. All of these can lead to a major crisis when the systems finally collapse.

Economic and market forces

With a global economy and high-speed information, markets and economies change far more rapidly than they did twenty years ago. These forces can change—or appear to change—quite swiftly. Consider these examples:

- **Market swings.** An unexpected spike or collapse in buying alters predicted sales, product development, and scheduling. Even though regular market swings can make for difficult times, a major disruption in markets results in crises.

- **Trends.** An overall change in consumer demand leaves backward-looking companies in the dust. The rise of the personal computer is an excellent example. Although it was not predicted, it became the new way of life in businesses and homes. Companies that believed that mainframe technology would always be the only market were caught unaware. And many of them went under.

- **Investment bubbles.** Periods of rampant speculation and investment frenzy blow business opportunities out of proportion until the economic realities cause the bubbles to burst. The instant deflation of portfolios, life savings, retirement incomes, and job opportunities creates crises for many.

Tip: Avoid ongoing financial crises by fully funding development projects from the beginning.

Business-relationship crises

All businesses depend on people within the company and outside it, including business partners, vendors, and customers. What does your company do when a crucial leader dies unexpectedly? When a subcontractor in charge of security allows a serious breach at a major airport? When a vendor fails to deliver critical supplies? When an employee is caught embezzling money from a client account? When a partner is indicted? When a major customer goes out of business? When two managers in your company become embroiled in a destructive personal conflict?

Tip: Avoid relationship crises by confronting and negotiating problems before they escalate.

What You COULD Do.

Remember Cal's concern about how to conduct a crisis audit?

Here's what the mentor suggests:

Cal might begin by talking with colleagues who work in different areas to better understand what might go wrong in tougher times. If you were responsible for a town dam, you would certainly perform an audit of its structural integrity before a storm caused the water to rise. Likewise, it is important for Cal to perform a crisis audit when things are going well at work so that he can be better prepared should a crisis arise. One of the first steps in performing a crisis audit is to talk with many different people within the organization to gather different perspectives of what could happen. Next, Cal should conduct a *SWOT analysis* to determine the company's *strengths, weaknesses, opportunities,* and *threats* for each potential crisis.

Six stages of crisis management

All crises—whether related to uncontrollable events, health, technology, changing markets, or business relationships—have the potential to affect your company's reputation, its bottom line, its people, and, ultimately, its ability to do business. Although there is no simple formula for eliminating crises, following the six stages of crisis management can make a big difference in how successfully *your* firm copes with crises.

The stages are as follows:

1. Avoiding the crisis

2. Preparing to manage the crisis

3. Recognizing the crisis

4. Containing the crisis

5. Resolving the crisis

6. Learning from the crisis

In the chapters that follow, we'll examine each of these stages in close detail.

Stage 1: Avoiding the Crisis

CRISES THAT ARE handled poorly often get the greatest media attention. But we don't often hear much about crises that were prevented. Remember the Y2K bug? On New Year's Day, 2000, virtually every computer in the world made the calendar switch to the new millennium without a hitch. All that those who were listening for trouble heard was the quiet sound of a crisis that had been prevented. For years, businesses had worked to solve the Y2K problem before it could strike. And their efforts paid off.

Of course, managers at every level of an organization intercede and prevent minor crises every day. For instance:

- A sales representative notices that a client's name is misspelled on every page of a major sales proposal. The manager has all the copies destroyed, makes the adjustments, and has new proposals printed at an all-night copy center, saving the company from losing a major account.

- A manager foresees a cash flow shortage, takes steps to hurry receivables, and makes sure a credit line is available at the company's bank should the expected cash still not come in.

- A team leader, when informed that a key employee is leaving, takes steps to find a replacement instead of leaving it to the last minute.

All these managers are actively involved in avoiding crises. It's their job. But to practice effective crisis avoidance, you need to take a disciplined approach. And that includes conducting a crisis audit and considering potential crises in the four major areas we discussed earlier.

Conducting a crisis audit

Most managers are already attuned to *possible* and *probable* crises and take some steps to avoid them. But you can become even more effective by preparing for crises when things are going well. The first step is to perform a crisis audit. Look for things that are going wrong now or that have the potential to go wrong in the future.

A crisis audit may look like one more "to do" on your already-long list, but it's an important part of your company's or department's long-term plan.

A crisis audit involves the following steps:

1. **Make crisis planning a part of your strategic planning.** Incorporate the crisis audit into your part of the overall strategic planning process. Whether you run your own business or department, you still have to plan strategically for the future, and that planning needs to include crisis planning.

2. **Get together and share ideas.** People's perspectives about potential crises often differ greatly. No one person has all the information a company needs. By talking to people from other areas of your department, division, or company, you may get some surprising information. Work with colleagues in your department and in other departments to analyze your situation.

3. **Perform a SWOT analysis.** One useful strategic planning tool is the *SWOT analysis* (strengths, weaknesses, opportunities, threats). Conduct the analysis specifically from a crisis perspective. After all, crises often evolve from internal weaknesses or external threats.

   For example, what are your organization's internal weaknesses? Where might a crisis occur in your normal business procedures? For example, are you so understaffed that if one member of the team were to leave, you couldn't function? Or is your infrastructure old and patched together? Are you having quality-control problems that could lead to consumer dissatisfaction or harm?

   And what are your most likely external threats? Which of those threats would be the most damaging to your company? For example, is your competition likely to introduce a radically new product, making yours obsolete?

   Note that many people refuse to recognize the one major threat that looms over the company. By ignoring the reality, any constructive action that might avert or lessen the impact of the problem is left undone. For example, if your company has been successfully producing one major product line, but the managers refuse to acknowledge a new, innovative product that will eventually make your entire product line obsolete, your company very likely will not survive.

4. **Focus on the four major crisis areas.** Consider potential health and environmental disasters, technological breakdowns, economic and market forces, and relationships.

5. **Narrow your crisis-risk list.** In performing the crisis audit, ask yourselves two basic questions: What are the *worst* things that could go wrong? What are the *most likely* or *probable* crises that could occur? You can't possibly address every potential problem or crisis, and some crises simply won't touch your organization. For example, if your company is not located in an earthquake zone, don't put earthquakes on your crisis-risk list. Or if you work at a consulting firm, you won't need to worry about a possible labor strike.

   Narrow your crisis-risk list by focusing on the crises that would have the worst result, would be most likely to occur, and would affect your group or company.

"Make a list of everything that could attract trouble to the business, consider the possible consequences, and estimate the cost of prevention."
   —Norman Augustine

Spotlight on the four major crisis areas

Trying to anticipate every possible type of crisis can be overwhelming. Let's look in more detail at how you focus on the four major crises areas.

- **Health and environmental disasters.** The health and safety of employees, consumers, the general public, and the environment are high priorities. This type of crisis can escalate from a small problem to a major crisis quickly, particularly when people within the institution try to cover it up, place blame, or minimize its importance.

- **Technological breakdowns.** You probably already have a good idea of some of the biggest weaknesses in your company's or department's technology. Maybe it's the phone system, the server, or the Internet connection. Weaknesses in technology can precipitate paralyzing crises if left untreated.

- **Economic and market forces.** Economic forces and market swings can be crises with the greatest opportunities hidden inside—but only if you are prepared. Otherwise, an unexpected market swing can be damaging or even devastating.

- **Relationships.** People are unpredictable. They may do things that you would not think possible, particularly if money or advancement is involved. Organizations with which you have partnered for a long time may also surprise you. Consider, for example, the advertising agency whose *Fortune* 500 client simply closed its doors. Millions of dollars' worth of business was lost. As a manager, you have to deal with numerous and diverse relationships. Look for vulnerable relationships. Be particularly aware of the one vendor, client, or computer whiz whose sudden departure could ruin your company.

Stage 2: Preparing to Manage the Crisis

N BUSINESS, CREATING a crisis-management plan means making as many decisions as you can before the crisis occurs, so that your energies can go into handling the crisis effectively *if and when it does occur*. Many of these tasks are fairly easy to do when things are going well, but difficult and stressful to do in the middle of a crisis.

However, just as a hospital arranges for a standby generator in case power goes out during surgery, you need backup plans for the set of crises you have identified as the ones your company or department must expect and prepare for.

Recognizing the risks and costs

Consider a major investment company that had only one line of business: helping individual investors buy and sell stocks. When the investment market was at its peak, this company did a booming business. It poured its profits into expanding its business by hiring more people and opening more offices. But when the economy stalled and individual investors stopped buying, the company had no other sources of revenue. The company's stock dropped, and it was forced to make huge layoffs—which affected everyone in the organization. By exploring other sources of revenue and investing some of its profits in those opportunities—and by doing some "what-ifs" about its rate of growth—the company might have lessened some effects of the disaster.

Use the results of your crisis audit as a basis from which to brainstorm potential crises. Question basic assumptions about your business—for both the present and the future. What assumptions do you have that *might* not be true? Ask yourself, "What would happen if people stopped buying our best-selling product?" or "What if demand for our product is so huge that we can't fill our orders?" It's important to do this as a group. Other people can provide a valuable perspective on each other's closely held assumptions. And finally ask, "How would this impact our group?"

Once you've determined what crises you need to plan for, consider ways to minimize these risks. Also, brainstorm the costs for each risk you've identified. Consider everything that might go wrong, and assess the costs if it should. A risk analysis measures more than just costs in terms of money. Determine costs in terms of human health and safety, and other important factors such as ability to meet customers' demands, ability of employees to work and communicate efficiently, and your company's reputation. Prioritize those risks that are most pressing and costly, and deal with them first.

Developing a crisis plan

After you have selected a key what-if scenario and analyzed possible consequences, brainstorm the kinds of decisions that will have to be made. For example, in the event of a natural disaster, employees may have to be evacuated, and second- or third-shift employees might have to be notified. If a problem arises in getting a product to market, additional staff may have to be hired quickly, alternative methods of transportation might have to be lined up, or management may have to answer phones. In the event of an impending strike by transportation workers, you might have to call in a team of employees who drive minivans to bring some people to work, and arrange for some people to work from home.

As you go through this exercise, start to consider who should be making these decisions. Also, perform a reality check on your plan by brainstorming possible unintended—and undesirable—side effects. For example, when a chain of auto-repair shops wanted to boost sagging sales, management offered mechanics sales incentives. The more work they brought in, the bigger bonus they'd make. Unfortunately, some of the mechanics began recommending unnecessary repairs. Customers complained that they were being ripped off, and the chain's reputation suffered. Similarly, a factory offered incentives for every defective product turned in, but it soon turned out that some workers were deliberately damaging products in order to receive the awards. And when a pizza company promised to deliver its "pizza in 30 minutes or it's free," speeding drivers caused car accidents.

You don't have to cover every eventuality, but thinking things through carefully can help prevent such unanticipated problems.

Forming a crisis-management team

The outcome of the crisis depends on the performance of the people making the decisions. The better prepared they are, the

Steps for Developing a Crisis Plan

1. **Identify obstacles and fail points.**

   What factors could make the crisis worse? Lack of staff? No evacuation plan? Technology? Weather? Lack of money? Lack of knowledge? Brainstorm obstacles and fail points, and then determine ways to deal with them.

2. **Create a resource plan.**

   Depending on the type of crisis, consider what you may need to resolve it. Then plan for those resources to be on hand when needed. For example, employees traveling to dangerous parts of the world may need quick access to cash. Determine what resources you need, how you will get them, and who will be in charge.

3. **Create a communication plan.**

   Decide who will need to know about the crisis—include both internal and external people. Then develop a communication plan so that each key person will be informed as needed. The communication plan could be as simple as an emergency contact list or a more complex communication tree designating the flow of messages.

4. **Distribute resource and communication plans.**

   Make sure all key people have and understand the resource and communication plans. Call a meeting to review the plans and go over each person's role during an emergency. A mock crisis drill could even be performed to test whether the plans will actually work.

better the crisis will be handled. Determine who on your team will:

- Be involved in handling each aspect of the crisis
- Make what kinds of decisions
- Notify authorities within the company
- Notify employees, government agencies, media, and so forth
- Decide whether employees should stay home
- Decide to evacuate a building
- Decide to hire temporary personnel in the event of an unexpected business rush

Once these decisions have been made, make sure that every person on the team has a backup in case they are unavailable.

In addition, create and distribute a list of all phone numbers, e-mail addresses, and ways to reach critical team members. Have people put the list on their computers, in their mobile-phone address books, on wireless communicators, and in their home offices . . . wherever anyone on the team could possibly need access to it.

Then, identify both formal and informal networks within the organization. Who are key players you may need to rely on in a crisis?

Creating a communications and resource plan

Create lists of all people who will need to be contacted in the event of a crisis—not just the members of the team—and how to contact them. You may need to include all employees, vendors, and customers.

Tip: Make it a point to establish relationships that you don't already have. When a crisis comes, it's a lot easier to handle if you already know all the players.

Also, for each crisis on your list, think about what resources will be needed to handle the situation. For example, if you manage a research project in a pharmaceutical firm, you may have to prepare for a biological or health-related crisis. If you are trying to develop a market niche in an underdeveloped country, your employees may be in real physical danger. In both these examples, the resources required would be very different—from a store of specific antidotes to a detailed escape plan.

Tip: In creating a crisis-communications plan, make a list of the five questions you would least like to be asked regarding the crisis. (Be assured that someone will ask them.) Prepare answers to the questions.

Stage 3:
Recognizing the
Crisis

THE CHIEF EXECUTIVE officer of a major corporation was alerted one day that the president of one of its subsidiaries—a film company—had been accused of embezzling money and forging checks. But the CEO refused to believe that the film-company president would ever commit such crimes. He ignored the problem, but it didn't go away. By the time the CEO decided to fire the president, the charismatic thief had gotten board members lined up on his side. The board insisted on keeping the president. The situation worsened, with reports coming out in the paper tarnishing the name of the film company, the corporation, and all involved—including the CEO. It was an ugly, painful crisis. And it could have been avoided if the chief had recognized it as a potential crisis and dealt with it promptly.

Like this CEO, many managers don't want to face unpleasant situations. Unfortunately, unpleasant situations can be signs of an impending crisis. Pay attention to that voice inside you that says, "Uh-oh, there's something wrong!" The CEO must have been very disturbed when he found out that his film-company president was accused of embezzling. But he rationalized the event by telling himself that what he had heard was impossible.

Is it a crisis?

On a day-to-day basis, managers learn of many disturbing facts and events. Instead of trying to ignore them, rationalize them, or minimize their importance, turn around and face them. Take a minute to step outside yourself and question the event and its consequences.

First, *characterize the event*. Use the checklist shown in the table "Is it a crisis?" to determine whether you're dealing with an impending crisis.

Second, *evaluate the size of the crisis*. Once you've realized that you are dealing with a crisis, determine its scope and magnitude.

Is it a crisis?

Has the event in question caused, or does it have the potential to cause . . .	Yes	No
Injury to any person?		
A threat to the health or safety of any person?		
A threat to the environment?		
A breakdown in your company's ability to serve customers or a threat to your company's reputation?		
A serious threat to employees' morale and well-being?		
A loss of data?		
Serious financial loss?		
A legal action against your company or an individual associated with it (employee, subcontractor, partner)?		
Interpreting your score: If you answered yes to any of the above questions, you are probably dealing with an impending crisis.		

Quickly gather as much information as you can. Ask yourself questions such as the following:

- How many people are involved? Who are they?
- How long is this likely to last?
- Have any laws been broken? If yes, which ones?
- Who already knows about the crisis? What do they know?
- Who needs to know?
- What are the costs already in terms of health? Money? Reputation?

Third, *self-reflect*. Evaluate how you might manage the situation. Are you someone who tends to underreact? If so, maybe you need to become more concerned. Or do you have a tendency to overreact? If yes, you may need to calm down.

Fourth, *consider your values*. What is important? What is the *right* thing to do? For example, if an employee is breaking the law—and using the company to do it—what is your responsibility? Or if a subcontractor is disposing of toxic waste from your company illegally, harming the environment and possibly endangering lives, and you suspect the company is turning a blind eye to it, what should you do?

If it is a crisis, how will you deal with it?

Suppose you've decided that you do have a crisis on your hands. What do you do? You may have to deal with some aspects of the situation immediately, but you will also need to come up with a flexible plan for dealing with the crisis's short- and long-term effects. The following strategies can help:

- **Get a team in place.** Assemble your crisis-management team as quickly as possible. Depending on the scope of the situation, members of the team may need to be assigned to the crisis full-time. If the crisis is big enough, or of long enough duration, you may need to pull the crisis-management team off some or all of their regular duties. If you have performed a crisis audit, then your team members will already know what their roles are and how to communicate with each other.

- **Get the information you need.** Throughout the crisis, you'll need key information about what's happening—as it happens. You'll need to ask the right people the right questions. Work with your team to make sure the information keeps flowing. You'll also need to make sense out of the information you get. Sort out what's relevant and what isn't, what's important and what's trivial. It's easy to get bogged down in details, so step back every now and then, and take a broad view of the situation.

- **Get a sounding board.** At this phase of the crisis, it's also important to have a sounding board—a person you can trust who will help you talk through ideas, information, and decisions.

Tip: If you've determined that you are facing
a crisis, get the facts as quickly as you can,
to the best of your ability.

Stage 4: Containing the Crisis

WHEN A CRISIS DOES strike, the first thing you must do is contain it. Your goal is to stop the hemorrhaging fast. You must make decisions quickly. Be on the scene. Your physical presence is important. It lets everyone know that your company cares about what is happening. And you must communicate critical information to key people.

For example, when a supermarket chain was accused by a major TV network of selling spoiled meat, the value of its stock plummeted. But the management team responded quickly. They gathered the facts by not only listening to the news media and hearing the message from stockholders but by paying attention to and working with their own employees as well.

They immediately stopped the practice of selling less-than-fresh meat, and they put large windows in the meat-preparation areas so the pubic could watch meat being packaged. They expanded their employee training, gave public tours of their facilities, and offered consumer discounts to draw people back into the stores. The company eventually earned an excellent rating from the Food and Drug Administration, and its sales returned to normal.

Demonstrating decisiveness and compassion

When a torrential rain flooded a section of a building, the water destroyed computers, carpeting, paper records, and the workspace of ten employees. The manager was on the scene as the workers showed up in the morning, to help them and to direct immediate cleanup efforts. After the cleanup, workers began having breathing problems and headaches. Though the carpet had been cleaned, it was determined that it was probably infested with mold. Instead of trying to clean the carpet again or waiting for budgetary approval, the manager immediately ordered all the carpet in the area to be removed and replaced.

This manager demonstrated two essential qualities necessary in a crisis: decisiveness and compassion. First, his presence on the scene showed that he, and the company, cared. Later, his decisiveness in replacing the toxic carpeting demonstrated that the health of employees was more important than any other consideration.

Decisiveness is not always easy, but it's important when you're containing a crisis. Often, you have to act on too little or inexact information. If there is no workable contingency plan in place, if there are no guidelines for the situation, and if there are no trusted confidants, there is still always your conscience. Ask yourself, "What's the right thing to do?" And then do it, hoping it is the right thing!

Compassion is a part of many organizations' cultures, and it is typically rewarded in those cultures. But not always. Some companies pride themselves on having a ruthless and competitive culture. Nevertheless, a manager still has the power to set the tone for his or her own division. No manager—regardless of the corporate culture—has to abandon compassion or humanity, especially during a crisis.

What Would YOU Do?

Stop That Leak

INDRA MANAGES THE IT department at DatServ, an information services company. One day, a technician from her group comes to her with troubling news: apparently, a hacker has broken into one of DatServ's customer databases and corrupted some of the information in it. Luckily, DatServ's tech staff has quickly reprogrammed the company's security software and recovered the damaged data. The staff has also reassured the affected customer that no permanent harm was done to its database. Indra decides also to review DatServ's security software, with an eye toward making any necessary changes to prevent further hacking.

However, news of the incident has spread throughout the industry. The affected DatServ customer tells other customers about the security breach. Equally alarming, a journalist calls Indra's department, looking for information. Apparently, someone has leaked word of the incident to an industry trade magazine.

Even though DatServ fixed the breach quickly and repaired the damage, it seems Indra now has a public relations disaster on her hands. She's got to say something about the situation to key people—including DatServ's top management, major customers, employees, and the media. But what?

What would YOU do? The mentor will suggest a solution in *What You COULD Do.*

Tip: While managing a crisis, acknowledge and show sympathy for human suffering.

Communicating about the crisis

Anyone who is handling a crisis is going to have to communicate about it with others. These others could be the general public or your immediate employees, vendors, suppliers, and clients. In any case, you will need to communicate to your direct reports how the crisis will impact them and what they need to do. What you say and how you say it are critical. You are managing the perceptions of people whose reactions can drastically affect what happens. The way you communicate can precipitate actions that can make the crisis worse—or better. A crisis, by definition, means that there is bad news. Dealing with pain and anger early on can forestall far worse problems later on. Your goal is to contain the overall crisis, not to make the present moment easier.

"One's objective should be to get it right,
get it quick, get it out, and get it over."
—Warren Buffett

When communicating during a crisis:

- **Expect rumors and false information.** During a crisis, people crave information—whether it's true or not. Use the communication strategy you've developed as part of your crisis planning to address and stop the flood of false news.

- **Notify key people.** Inform anyone who needs to know—company management, customers, employees, suppliers, government authorities—and do so quickly, within two hours, if possible. If you have created a communication plan or list of important phone numbers, now is the time to use it.

- **Stick to the facts.** Whether you're talking to coworkers, authorities, or the media, make your message straightforward and honest. Avoid these typical, but inappropriate messages: "No comment." "We haven't read the complaint." "A mistake was made." Give all the facts that you know. You are not obligated to speculate or to cover up, because lying and speculating will only damage your credibility and your company's credibility if and when you are proved wrong. Moreover, communicate all the bad news at once. It's like pulling off a sticky bandage. It will hurt now, but it will be over soon.

Tip: Record a voice message on a phone line at the end of each day, so that people can call and hear what is really going on. Your voice is a powerful communications tool. Also, use a Web site to gather and post important information. Your company Web site has credibility and is easily accessible by everyone.

?hat You COULD Do.

Remember Indra's dilemma about what to say to the media (as well as DatServ's management, customers, and employees) about the security breach?

Here's what the mentor suggests:

In communicating to these various constituencies about the security breach, Indra should convey all the bad news at the same time (rather than doling it out in small pieces). Moreover, she should tell people everything she knows about what happened. By taking this approach, she comes across as open and honest. Journalists and other stakeholders won't conclude that she's hiding something, and they won't feel compelled to keep digging for more "dirt." Though this approach can be painful—like pulling off a sticky bandage all at once—the pain will end much sooner than if Indra were to omit or cover up key facts.

Additional suggestions for Indra include preparing carefully for any press conference or presentation, being honest about what she knows and doesn't know, and accepting responsibility for handling the crisis (not causing it). She should also avoid promising anything that she can't deliver. (It is wiser to underpromise and then deliver more, than to overpromise and come up short.) Finally, Indra should resist any urge to qualify expressions of sympathy (e.g., "We're sorry this happened, *but* . . .").

Stage 5: Resolving the Crisis

B Y DEFINITION, A crisis requires fast, confident decision making. But how do you make good decisions when events are moving quickly, when things are confusing, and when it's hard to sort out what's important? How can you stay on track? Managing the emotions that accompany a crisis, understanding the leader's role, and taking effective action can help.

Managing the emotions

Typically, three emotions can combine to create stress for everyone experiencing a crisis:

- Fear of disaster

- Anticipation of a potentially positive outcome

- Desire for the crisis to be over

Under stress, you feel the pressure to make a decision. But the pressure can push you to a state of panic where you are making decisions solely to be "doing something." In reality, however, you are dispersing energy and resources—and this energy is your source of strength. Use the power of positive stress to handle the crisis as a confident leader.

Try to avoid "toxic" stress responses. Often, people respond to these natural and conflicting feelings of fear, hope, and despair in ways that can aggravate—rather than relieve—the crisis. Consider these examples of common ineffective and often harmful responses:

- **When in doubt, scream and shout.** Making noise may give you the feeling that you're doing something, but it wastes energy and won't resolve the crisis.

- **Hide your head in the sand.** At times, the pressure to act becomes so stressful that a manager slips into a state of paralysis and can't make any decisions at all.

TOXIC STRESS RESPONSE *n* **1:** a response to the emotions triggered by a crisis that aggravates rather than relieves the crisis

---

How to handle your uncertainty and fear during a crisis? Use the energy you derive from these emotions to face the crisis and deal with it as effectively as possible. In addition, adapt your response according to whether the crisis is sudden or long-running. For example, if the crisis flares up and is over quickly, then try these simple steps to maintain your emotional balance.

1. **Stop.** As soon as you begin to feel the first rush of anxiety flooding your mind, say "Stop!" to yourself. To face a crisis, you need to have a clear mind as unclouded by anxiety, toxic stress, and fear as possible. Thus, recognizing those feelings and verbally pushing back can block them from controlling your mind and actions.

2. **Breathe.** Take a deep breath. Just as the word *stop* blocks the negative thoughts from your mind, breathing overcomes the stress-induced tendency to hold your breath.

3. **Reflect.** By interrupting the pattern of toxic stress and giving yourself energy through breathing, you can now focus on the *real* problem: the crisis you face. By reflecting on your stress response, you can begin to distinguish the different levels of thought and to sort out reasonable from irrational stress responses. You can see the practical situation more calmly and realistically and distinguish it from the distortions of your anxiety-influenced thoughts.

4. **Choose.** With your attention now on the practical situation itself, you can choose to find real solutions, follow the crisis plan your group has developed, and tend to the needs of the people you lead.

Some crises start as a slow burn and then break out into a wildfire of trouble. For example, financial crises often begin as small problems in a company's receivables or perhaps cash flow fluctuations. Then they build to an inability to borrow or cover basic expenses. You may have a sense of the emerging crisis for several weeks or months, yet you're unable to stop the spread of trouble.

During this kind of crisis, when you're coping with stress over long periods of time, taking care of yourself becomes even more important. Long-term stress can be toxic—physically harmful to you. Taking care of yourself gives you the strength and stamina to take care of the impact of the crisis. So even when you feel hemmed in by the growing crisis, remember to:

- Talk to people—don't become isolated

- Get enough sleep

- Exercise regularly

- Eat a balanced diet

- Avoid alcohol, caffeine, and sugar

- Take a break whenever you can

- Find humor wherever you can

Understanding the leader's role

Whether as the CEO of a large corporation or a supervisor of a department, an effective leader finds out as quickly as possible what the real problem is during a crisis. Often, there will be a flurry of information, most of it inaccurate. It's your task to discover the truth and face it by asking the right people, listening to the most reliable voices, and going to the right places.

A leader in a crisis responds by:

- **Facing the crisis**—turning fear into positive action

- **Being vigilant**—watching for new developments and recognizing the importance of new information

- **Maintaining focus on the priorities**—ensuring that people are safe first, and then assessing the next most critical needs

- **Assessing and responding** to what is in his or her control and ignoring what is not

Taking action

As a leader, you take action on several fronts to resolve the crisis:

- **Activate your crisis plan.** Once you understand the problem, there are probably only a few realistic options open to you. If you have a crisis plan in place, use it.

- **Help everyone work together.** A leader has the power to draw people together to act as a team. If your people know you are in charge, they will respond to your direction.

- **Avoid blaming others.** As the crisis heats up, the impulse to blame people can become irresistible. Certainly, a team member's incompetence or serious error may have caused the crisis, or it may be perpetuating it. However, during the heat of the crisis, trying to find a scapegoat is counterproductive. Focus your people on handling the crisis, not on blaming others. Later, after the crisis, it will be up to you to analyze whether a person should be reprimanded in some way. However, keep in mind that constant faultfinding lowers morale and stifles the creativity and commitment you need to solve the problem. Create an atmosphere where people look forward to what needs to be done, not backward to who was at fault.

- **Do what needs to get done.** Rules, policies, structures, procedures, and budgets are created to maintain order and provide a productive process in the normal course of business. However, most rules were not created with a crisis in mind. Do whatever has to be done, and don't worry about the "rules."

Consider this example of how a leader took effective action during a crisis. When a catalog retailer that offered a large number of custom products—monogrammed bags, sweaters, and so forth—put out its holiday catalog, it was shocked by the positive response. From the moment the catalog was released in October, the company's phone lines were swamped. The retailer hired temporary help to work the phones, but still had a tremendous bottleneck: customizing and shipping the products. It was the holiday season. The head of distribution recognized that if they didn't get everything shipped in time for the holidays, there might not be a next season.

So the CEO put out a call for help and recruited management and administrative staff to work in the warehouse in the evenings—after they had done their regular jobs. Everyone worked together for six long and grueling weeks—everyone from the top down. By working as a team, the whole company eventually enjoyed astonishing success by growing 80 percent in that one year. What could have been a crisis and failure was turned around by teamwork.

Tip: Determine who can help you handle the crisis, and bring them together immediately. You may need to create a team whose job it is to handle the crisis, while others in your department or business are charged with running business as usual.

Stage 6: Learning from the Crisis

WHEN YOU SURVIVE a crisis, don't just try to put it behind you. Rather, take the opportunity to learn from the experience and make changes to avoid or prepare for another similar event. Engineers, for instance, use earthquakes as a learning experience to plan for stronger roads, bridges, and buildings. They use massive floods to determine the best ways for people to adapt to the power of nature (build dams or dikes) or yield to that power (move out of a flood plain).

You, too, can do a postcrisis audit to learn and even profit from the event. For example, when everyone in the catalog company worked overtime to fill a large volume of orders they hadn't expected to receive, they successfully handled the immediate crisis. But operating in crisis mode is an ineffective way to work all the time. It takes its toll on morale, turnover, and the health of everyone, especially the manager. After the rush at the catalog company, people were given large bonuses and extra vacation time. Then management took steps to plan for the next year, so the company would be prepared to meet a large demand—with less pressure on the employees.

POSTCRISIS AUDIT *n* **1:** a review of what happened during a crisis and how people responded, designed to enable the organization to learn from the event

---

Reviewing how the crisis was handled

Plan the timing of the crisis review soon enough after the event so that people remember details, but long enough afterward for some emotional healing to have taken place. Start by analyzing the crisis from beginning to end. Pinpoint actions, assumptions, and outside factors that precipitated the crisis. Ask yourself the following questions:

- Knowing what we knew then, could we have prevented the crisis? If so, how?

- At what point did we realize we were in a crisis? Could we have recognized the signs earlier?

- What warning signals went off that we may have ignored?

- What warning signals did we pay attention to?

- What were the early signs? Why were they turning points?

- What did we do right? What could we have done better?

- What were the stress points in the system that failed?

Planning for the next one

Knowing what you know now, how can you prevent the same type of crisis from occurring again? Create a plan so that you learn from what you know.

- **Get input from everyone.** You need to get everyone's story, but pay attention in particular to those with expertise in the areas of importance. If the crisis was technological, then listen to the computer experts, the IT group, the network engineers. If the crisis was relational—a critical vendor cuts off your supply of goods—talk to your buyers, but then go out in the field and find out what happened and why.

- **Incorporate the ideas and information in your next round of strategic planning.** You've already performed your first crisis audit. Now you'll have much more knowledge to improve the revised audit and the crisis-prevention plan.

Successful managers make each crisis a learning experience. For example, the catalog company experienced a crisis when its phone lines were swamped after the release of its holiday catalog. Management listened to employees and outside consultants. Consultants analyzed workflow, looking at bottlenecks and technology. And everyone in the company who had worked in the warehouse to help get through the crunch now understood firsthand how the business was run. Their experience had taught everyone a great deal. The CEO set up a system to tap into the cumulative knowledge of the company's workforce. The firm set up a suggestion program and put many resulting ideas into practice. Each quarter, it gave a $100 reward to the employee who came up with the best idea.

Tip: Break the crisis down into component parts, to analyze how you might handle a similar crisis more effectively next time. If you look at the problem as one big tidal wave, you will find it more difficult to learn from the experience.

Tracking results

Track the results of changes you make after the crisis. How are they working? Will they actually reduce the negative impact of a future event? For example, as a result of a comprehensive analysis and much planning, the catalog company was well prepared for the next season. Some of the realizations and improvements that were generated by the analysis included those shown in the table "Tracking results."

Tracking results

Problem identified	Action taken
The outdated IT system was incapable of handling the large volume of business.	The system was redesigned and overhauled. The division grew from one of the smallest in the company to one of the largest.
There were too many colors for customizable items, which caused delays in processing orders.	The number of colors offered was reduced; offerings were streamlined.
Most of the orders came in a three-month period, while it was slow the rest of the year.	More catalogs were offered throughout the year.
Many shoppers ordered at the last minute, creating enormous demand on resources at one time.	To spread out the frequency of demand, incentives were offered to encourage customers to order earlier in the season.
Too many catalogs went out at once.	The release of catalogs and ability to respond was tracked, so that systems were always in place to handle demand.

Tips and Tools

Tools for
Managing Crises

The "10 Worst Things That Could Happen" List

Some managers find it helpful to create and have available a list of the ten worst things that could happen at work and what they would do about them. Use this tool to record your own list or have a team or work group develop their list.

Situation	What I/We Would Do About It
1.	
2.	
3.	
4.	
5.	
6.	
7.	
8.	
9.	
10.	

Emergency Contact List

Be sure to include all internal and external people who need to be notified during a crisis.

Name:				
Home Address:				
Work Phone	**Home Phone**	**Cell Phone**	**E-mail Address**	**Fax Number**

Name:				
Home Address:				
Work Phone	**Home Phone**	**Cell Phone**	**E-mail Address**	**Fax Number**

Name:				
Home Address:				
Work Phone	**Home Phone**	**Cell Phone**	**E-mail Address**	**Fax Number**

Name:				
Home Address:				
Work Phone	**Home Phone**	**Cell Phone**	**E-mail Address**	**Fax Number**

Name:				
Home Address:				
Work Phone	**Home Phone**	**Cell Phone**	**E-mail Address**	**Fax Number**

Name:				
Home Address:				
Work Phone	**Home Phone**	**Cell Phone**	**E-mail Address**	**Fax Number**

Name:				
Home Address:				
Work Phone	**Home Phone**	**Cell Phone**	**E-mail Address**	**Fax Number**

Name:				
Home Address:				
Work Phone	**Home Phone**	**Cell Phone**	**E-mail Address**	**Fax Number**

Name:				
Home Address:				
Work Phone	**Home Phone**	**Cell Phone**	**E-mail Address**	**Fax Number**

Name:				
Home Address:				
Work Phone	**Home Phone**	**Cell Phone**	**E-mail Address**	**Fax Number**

Name:				
Home Address:				
Work Phone	**Home Phone**	**Cell Phone**	**E-mail Address**	**Fax Number**

Name:				
Home Address:				
Work Phone	**Home Phone**	**Cell Phone**	**E-mail Address**	**Fax Number**

Additional Notes

Precrisis Resource Planning

What can you do now to make things easier later? Use this checklist to brainstorm about resources you might need in the event of a potential crisis. This information can also form the basis for a crisis action plan.

Describe the Crisis

Resources Required

Money

How much money would be needed? _____   Person in charge? _____
In what form? _____   What can be done now? _____
How will it be accessed? _____   _____

Medical Help

Who or where? _____   Person in charge? _____
Insurance information? _____   What can be done now? _____
How to contact? _____   _____

Transportation

Type of transportation? _____   From where to where? _____
For what purpose? _____   Under what likely conditions? _____
For how many? _____   Person in charge? _____
For whom? _____   What can be done now? _____

Legal Help

Name of law firm or attorney? _____   Person in charge? _____
Type of legal help? _____   What can be done now? _____

Temporary Help

Skills needed? _____   Length of employment? _____
Name of agency? _____   Person in charge? _____
Number of people? _____   What can be done now? _____

Governmental Help

Name of agency? _____   Person in charge? _____
Name and number of contact? _____   What can be done now? _____

Media Help

Designated spokesperson? _____   Person in charge? _____
Public relations agency? _____   What can be done now? _____
Media insider? _____   _____

Other Required Resources

Scenario Impact Assessment

Use this form to explore the potential consequences of a crisis. By thinking through a scenario and exploring "what-if" situations, you can better prepare to act with confidence if that situation or crisis should arise. Be sure to concentrate first or most on high-risk situations.

Identify a high-level crisis according to the following assessment:

High-risk-level crisis = high impact on the company plus high probability of occurring

	LOW	MEDIUM	HIGH
Potential impact of crisis on company	☐	☐	☐
Probability of crisis occurring	☐	☐	☐
Risk level of crisis	☐	☐	☐

Briefly Describe the Scenario

What could happen? _____
Who would be involved? _____
Where? _____
What would be the worst possible consequences? _____
What is the probability that this situation will occur? _____

Assess the Risk Level of the Scenario	Rating
How much does this situation have the potential to:	Low High 1 2 3 4 5
Endanger the health or safety of others?	
Cause loss of life and/or long-term harm to human health?	
Cause harm to the environment?	
Affect business-as-usual in your department or your business?	
Damage your department or your business's industry or public reputation?	
Have a significant financial impact?	
Trigger negative media attention, legal action, or governmental scrutiny?	
Damage employee relations or morale or contribute to employee turnover?	

List Other Potential Negative Impacts

Implications for Action

Given your responses to the above set of questions, are there certain preventative actions that can be taken now to lessen the negative impact of this scenario? Is there a plan in place to deal effectively and decisively with the worst consequences?

Capturing Learning from the Crisis

When the crisis is finally over, it's tempting to just put the whole thing behind you and move on. But a valuable learning opportunity will be lost. Use this form to capture some of the learning that you, your team, division, or company gleaned from experiencing the crisis. Break down each problem you faced, how you handled it, and what you learned. Then figure out how to prevent a similar problem from reoccurring and/or how to respond to it more effectively.

Crisis or Problem	Action Taken	What We Learned	Preventative Action
Example: *Key executive suddenly left to join another company.*	*We rushed into a disorganized search for a replacement.*	*We were unprepared and didn't know what our criteria were in our search. The process took too long.*	*Develop a succession plan for every key position in the company.*

Summary

In what ways did we handle the crisis effectively? How can we be sure to incorporate these positive actions into our crisis-management plans?

In what ways did we mishandle the crisis? What were the negative effects of our actions? How can we improve our crisis management in the future?

Test Yourself

This section offers ten multiple-choice questions to help you identify your baseline knowledge of crisis-management essentials. Answers to the questions are given at the end of the test.

1. You've just been assigned the task of preventing crises that could cause great harm to your organization. What's the first thing you do?

  a. Identify the crises that would cause most harm.
  b. Identify the crises that would be most likely.
  c. Form a crisis-analysis team.

2. A key employee has just informed you that his wife has a terminal illness. After expressing your sympathy and concern, what do you do?

  a. Find out how long she is expected to live.
  b. Work with him and other employees to create a flexible work plan.
  c. Encourage him to take a leave of absence.

3. True or false: When you are analyzing the potential damage a crisis can cause, the bottom line is the most important factor to consider.

  a. True.
  b. False.

4. What percentage of companies that experience a major data loss survive that crisis?

   a. Less than 10 percent.

   b. Between 10 percent and 30 percent.

   c. More than 30 percent.

5. Which type of crisis actually contains the greatest potential for business opportunity?

   a. A public-safety disaster.

   b. A technological breakdown.

   c. A market swing.

6. An internal accountant informs you that your highly paid staff member (with whom you have a friendly relationship) may be embezzling small sums of money. What do you do?

   a. Tell the accountant that the employee makes too much money to steal such small amounts.

   b. Discuss the situation with the employee offline, as a subtle warning to stop the embezzling in case it happens to be true.

   c. Examine the books closely with the accountant. If something's amiss, call in an auditor.

7. Which of the following organizational cultures would likely be most responsive to and effective in handling a crisis?

   a. A competitive culture where decisions get made and the job gets done no matter what.

b. A friendly culture based on trust.

c. A culture where information is closely protected and decisions are made at the top.

8. A disaster has just struck your company, and you are the designated spokesperson. A press conference will take place in one hour. How are you and your staff preparing to handle it?

a. You are writing a carefully worded statement revealing only what is about to become public knowledge.

b. You are writing a confident stating putting the most positive outlook on the problem and solutions.

c. You are preparing honest answers to the five questions you would least like to be asked.

9. You are the project manager on a key product for your company. Early results from user testing are mixed. You must still deliver within your deadline and on budget, but you don't know what to do about the mixed results. What is your first step?

a. Set up a flexible production team that can quickly make changes to the product indicated by focus tests.

b. Step back from the project. Analyze the information you're getting, to see what the problem really is.

c. Continue supporting the vision that began development of the product. Go about business as usual, creating an atmosphere of confidence and calm.

10. A crisis is finally over, and everyone feels both relieved and weary. Though you're tempted to get on with life, you know that you must assess what went wrong in order to prevent it from happening again. Where do you start?

   a. Get input from everyone involved to create a plan for the future.

   b. Determine who caused the problem and discipline him or her.

   c. Work with one or two key players to create a plan for the future.

Answers to test questions

1, c. Putting together a crisis-analysis team comprising a group of experienced people with different perspectives will give you an excellent start. Make the team a formal one with assigned tasks. A "watercooler" chat will not give you the depth or breadth you need to prevent and manage crises.

2, b. Your employee may want and need to work during the crisis, and may be very capable of performing on a part-time basis. Bringing people together during this crisis can help create the emotional support your employee will need to get through it.

3, b. A crisis has the potential to damage the health and safety of employees, your company's reputation, and your ability to serve customers—all equal in importance to the organization's bottom line.

4, a. A University of Texas study found that only 6 percent of companies that undergo major data loss survive the crisis. The good news is that this is one crisis that an organization can avoid relatively easily.

5, c. Changes in the market can spell disaster *or* growth for a company, depending on how well the organization predicts and handles such changes.

6, c. By examining the books with your accountant and calling in an independent auditor if something is amiss, you investigate the facts as quickly and objectively as possible—which is important to do in any crisis.

7, b. A company that values trust and compassion and that has created informal networks for the exchange of information can most easily demonstrate the team spirit and open communication needed to survive a crisis.

8, c. People are going to ask you tough questions whether you like it or not. You're better off being prepared with honest answers, even if the answer is "I don't know."

9, b. You can't solve a problem until you've clearly identified what it is. Once you've isolated the problem, you can break it down into component parts and decide how to resolve the situation.

10, a. Everyone who was affected by the crisis has a valuable perspective on what went wrong and ideas for how to prevent a similar crisis. Get input from all these individuals before making new plans.

To Learn More

Articles

Argenti, Paul. "Crisis Communication: Lessons from 9/11." *Harvard Business Review* (December 2002).

In this article, executives from a range of industries talk about how their companies, including Morgan Stanley, Oppenheimer Funds, American Airlines, Verizon, the New York Times, Dell, and Starbucks, went about restoring operations and morale after the terrorist attack of 9/11. From his interviews with these individuals, author and management professor Paul Argenti was able to distill a number of lessons, each of which, he says, may "serve as guideposts for any company facing a crisis that undermines its employees' composure, confidence, or concentration."

Augustine, Norman R. "Reshaping an Industry: Lockheed Martin's Survival Story." *Harvard Business Review* (November–December 1997).

In this behind-the-scenes story about the effects of the end of the Cold War on industry, Augustine draws important lessons about what industries can do to avoid crises and manage them once they begin.

Harvard Business School Publishing. "How to Keep a Crisis from Happening." *Harvard Management Update* (December 2000).

This article contains concise, practical information on how to prevent a crisis and how to handle one while it's occurring.

Harvard Business School Publishing. "Managing a Crisis." *Harvard Management Update* (August 2005).

This article explores the three emotions that combine during a crisis: fear of disaster, anticipation of a potentially positive outcome, and a desire for the crisis to be over. Each pulls you in a different emotional direction; together they create a distinct feeling of stress. And under stress, you feel the pressure to make a decision. But the pressure can push you to make decisions solely to be "doing something." Thus, people often respond to crises in ways that can aggravate rather than relieve the crisis. The authors explain how to avoid these futile and often harmful responses.

Mitroff, Ian I., and Murat C. Alpaslan. "Preparing for Evil." *Harvard Business Review* (April 2003).

The authors show how crisis-prepared companies use a systematic approach to focus their efforts. In addition to planning for natural disasters, they divide man-made calamities into two sorts: accidental ones, like the *Exxon Valdez* oil spill, and deliberate ones, like product tampering. Then they take steps to broaden their thinking about such potential crises. They imagine themselves as terrorists, for instance, or consider threats that would be common in other industries. And they seek creative outside input from investigative journalists, lawyers, and even reformed criminals.

Books

Deming, W. Edwards. *Out of the Crisis*. Cambridge, MA: MIT Press, 2000.

According to W. Edwards Deming, American companies require nothing less than a transformation of management style and of governmental relations with industry. In *Out of the Crisis*, originally published in 1986, Deming offers a theory of management based on his famous 14 Points for Management. Management's failure to plan for the future, he claims, brings about loss of market, which brings about loss of jobs. Management must be judged not only by the quarterly dividend, but by innovative plans to stay in business, protect investment, ensure future dividends, and provide more jobs through improved product and service. In simple, direct language, he explains the principles of management transformation and how to apply them.

Grove, Andrew S. *Only the Paranoid Survive: How to Exploit the Crisis Points That Challenge Every Company*. New York: Bantam Books, 1999.

Andrew Grove, chairman of Intel Corporation, outlines his inside experience and the ups and downs of Intel. He gives the reader a great inside look at the way change from every quarter can affect a major corporation, and he shares his vision in practical, direct language for capitalizing on change and crisis.

Harvard Business School Publishing. *Harvard Business Review on Crisis Management*. Boston: Harvard Business School Press, 1999.

This collection of eight essays highlights leading ideas on how to deal with difficult situations, crises, and other sensitive topics in a business environment. Obtaining the managerial skills and tools to effectively manage or avoid these crises is critical to the survival and success of your organization. In the lead article, "Managing the Crisis You Tried to Prevent," Norman Augustine uses his extensive personal experience in many executive situations to break down crises into predictable stages, with advice on how to handle each one. Other articles in this compilation give practical advice from frontline people on such topics as layoffs, product recalls, executive defection, media policy, and leadership.

Hurst, David K. *Crisis and Renewal: Meeting the Challenge of Organizational Change*. Boston: Harvard Business School Press, 2002.

Hurst presents a radically different view of how organizations evolve and renew themselves. The author tracks a cross-section of enterprises from their creative beginnings through the institutionalization of their success. Using a model of organizational ecocycles, he argues that managers need to create deliberate crises to preserve their organizations from destruction and to renew them with creativity and meaning.

Sources for Managing Crises

We would like to acknowledge the sources we used in developing this topic.

Augustine, Norman R. "50 Signs of Trouble—A List by Norman Augustine." Unpublished.

Augustine, Norman R. "Managing the Crisis You Tried to Prevent." *Harvard Business Review* OnPoint Enhanced Edition (2002).

Augustine, Norman R. Personal communication. November 2001.

Bureau of Labor Statistics.

Carlone, Katie. Personal communication. January 2002.

Dutton, Jane E., Peter J. Frost, Monica C. Worline, Jacoba M. Lilius, and Jason M. Kanov. "Leading in Times of Trauma." *Harvard Business Review* (January–February 2002).

Fink, Steven. *Crisis Management—Planning for the Inevitable.* New York: American Management Association, 1986.

Harvard Business School Publishing. *Manager's Toolkit.* Boston: Harvard Business School Press, 2004.

"How to Keep a Crisis from Happening." *Harvard Management Update* (December 2000).

Mitroff, Ian I., Christine M. Pearson, and L. Katharine Harrington. *The Essential Guide to Managing Corporate Crises.* Oxford: Oxford University Press, 1996.

"Read This, Then Go Back Up Your Data." *Fortune,* Special Tech Edition (Winter 2002).

Silva, Michael, and Terry McGann. *Overdrive—Managing in Crisis-Filled Times.* New York: John Wiley & Sons, 1995.

Sontag, Sherry, and Christopher Drew. "Blind Man's Bluff: The Untold Story of American Submarine Espionage." *Public Affairs* (1998).

Van Der Heijden, Kees. *Scenarios—The Art of Strategic Conversation.* New York: John Wiley & Sons, 1996.

Vernon, Lillian, with Catherine Fredman. "Too Much of a Good Thing." *United Airlines Hemispheres* (November 2001).

Vogelstein, Fred. "Can Schwab Get Its Mojo Back?" *Fortune* (September 17, 2001).

Wack, Pierre. "Scenarios: Uncharted Waters Ahead." *Harvard Business Review* (September–October 1985).

Notes

Notes

Notes

Notes

Notes

Notes

Notes

Notes

Notes

How to Order

Harvard Business Press publications are available worldwide from your local bookseller or online retailer.

You can also call:
1-800-668-6780

Our product consultants are available to help you 8:00 a.m.–6:00 p.m., Monday–Friday, Eastern Time. Outside the U.S. and Canada, call: 617-783-7450.

Please call about special discounts for quantities greater than ten.

You can order online at:
www.HBSPress.org